afon wysg: our river usk

y mynydd du sees rising bright
a rivulet reflect welsh light
black mountain slopes are on the cusp
of our meandering silver usk

through marshy sedge and upland peat
she courses, flowing, at their feet
fragments tumbling, nutrient rich
the start of food for nascent fish

lamprey, bullhead, shad and twait
live out their lives in hidden state
by bog, and marsh, and wand'ring wide
her water flows, a ribboned glide

on stone, a dipper bobs a while
while ripples split, and eddies smile
steps underwater, hunting fast
a caddis-fly with shadow cast

it's march, and round her gravel beds
if free of silt, the egg-filled redds
as darkness falls, and in the shade
dispersing fry swim unafraid

First published in the UK in 2023 by
A Blackbird Sang
Dene Edge, Laughton Hill, Stonesfield,
Oxfordshire, OX29 8DY, UK
www.ablackbirdsang.com

ALL TEXT © 2022 Tony Davis
ALL DRAWINGS © 2021 Kath Fotheringham
ICE-BAUBLE DRAWING © 2023 Jemima Brooke-Little

ISBN 978-1-7394068-0-6

DESIGN: Tony Davis and Kath Fotheringham
ARTWORK PHOTOGRAPHY: Darrin Roles

A CIP record of this book is available from the British
Library.

Printed by Pureprint Group, an ISO14001, FSC and
CarbonNeutral® accredited printing company.

This book was printed using 100% vegetable-based inks
and a water-based coating, on Revive 100 Uncoated,
a fully recycled paper.

River

an exploration in charcoal drawings,
word origins, dialect, and poetry

Drawings: Kath Fotheringham

Words: Tony Davis

rain

moss-boil

MOSS-BOIL n. (Galloway, Scotland). Large moorland fountains, the sources of rivers.

bourn

burn

BURN n. mall stream, Old English burna; related Old Norse brunnr, Lithuanian briáutis to burst forth.

runlet

gill

BOURN(E) n. a stream, esp an intermittent one in chalk areas.

KELD n. Also in form kell 1. A spring of water; a fountain; a marshy place. n. 2. The still part of a lake or river, which has an oily smoothness while the rest of the water is ruffled.

keld

rivulet

beck

BECK, n. 1. A brook, a small stream or river.

brook

strinn

STRIN(N) n. and vb. 1. n. A thin narrow stream of water; the channel of a river, etc. 2. vb. To flow in a thin, narrow stream.

fleet

millstream

WEIR, n. In comp. 1. Weir-hole, into which back-water of a mill-stream flows. 2. Weir-stead, place where there's a weir. 3. Pond or water pool, connected with a river; a ditch made to prevent the overflowing of water.

weir

waterway

ness

sluice

clow

CLOW, n. 1. The outfall sluice of a river or drain linking with a tidal river; a sluice or flood-gate in a mill-dam, watercourse.

spillway

stream

river

BACKWATER, n. 1. Water near the side of a river, which, when the current is strong, flows contrary way to the stream. 2. A stream from the sea. 3. The still or dead water that rises in a field during a river flood.

backwater

trink

TRINK, n. Also written trinck and in forms trenk; trinkie Shetland Isles 1. n. A narrow, open drain for the passage of water; narrow channel between rocks on the sea-coast; the bed or channel of a river or stream; the water which flows in the channel.

BROAD, n. An extensive piece of water formed by the broadening out of a river.

broad

estuary

sea

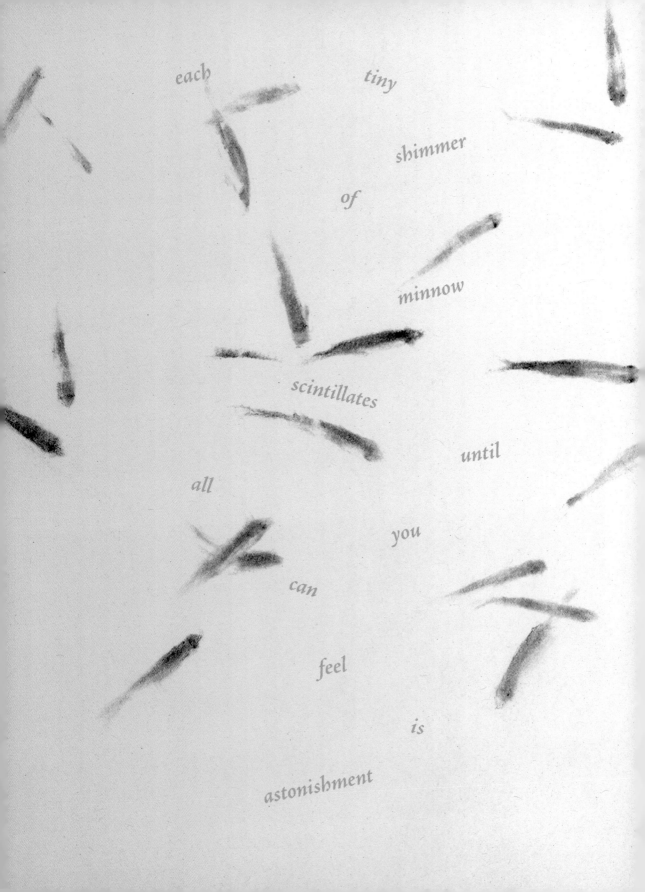

each   *tiny*

shimmer

of

minnow

scintillates

until

all

you

can

feel

is

astonishment

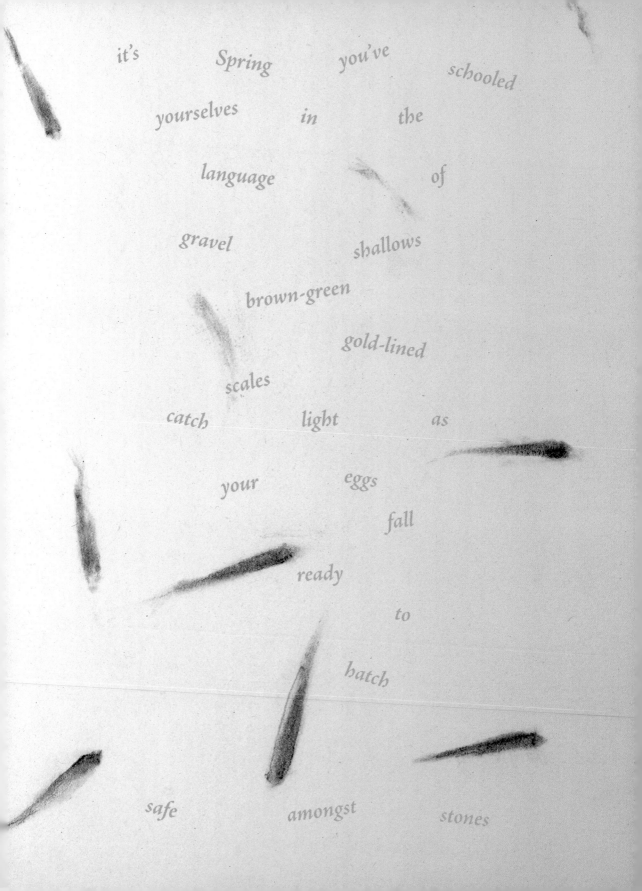

it's   Spring   you've   schooled

yourselves   in   the

language   of

gravel   shallows

brown-green

gold-lined

scales

catch   light   as

your   eggs

fall

ready

to

hatch

safe   amongst   stones

heron

if
you
stand
for
long
enough
at
the
synaptic
bankside
of
this
bent-legged
mind
you'll
chance
upon
Heron
the Hunter
still
waiting
for
you
    better
    hope
    you're
    not
    a
      fish

anser
boomer
cran
fisher
frank
hearnshaw
jack
jenny
johnny
kitty
moll-hern
nanny
shederow
starch
tommy
wader
willock

emerald pepper pod
now two pairs of wings, and look!
darting dragonfly

adder breeze bull chaffinger coach-horse devil's darning needle flying esk granny's needle
heather-bill hobby-horse hornet hoss-stinger jacky-breezer king-fisher merry-maid
nadder-servant sanging-eather silver-pin snakes-stang stingy-bob tom-breeze yedward

Dragonfly

the
wingspan
of all your
ancestors
would scare
us both but
you are scary
enough for
any prey you
chance to
snatch upon
the wing in
the briefest
blink of your
compound eye
they've gone
their bodies
consumed
their wings
clipped fall
lighter now
than air
down to
the flowing
stream
below

Flinders Petrie found a blue-glazed faience amulet of you from your ancestors in ancient Egypt. You are a medicine creature to many Native American tribes with special powers.

The Navajo say you symbolise pure water. And this is what you need. In Japan you are a creature of courage, strength and happiness. There are almost as many haiku about you as there are you.

In Sweden you are used to weigh people's souls. Lord Tennyson described you flitting your old skin and emerging shining metallic blue like sapphire mail. You are a constant wonder.

you disappeared
almost as fast as my eyes opened
a peremptory squatter
by mossy bankside

Even though you smiled
nacred teeth and scales
You'll never get me to eat sushi
look at me

furlessly challenging you
two feet away
I am houndless, but still
I would give my mind's eye teeth
to catch you
to prove it to everyone

a last glance,
fish in mouth
more than words
passes between us
before you slide

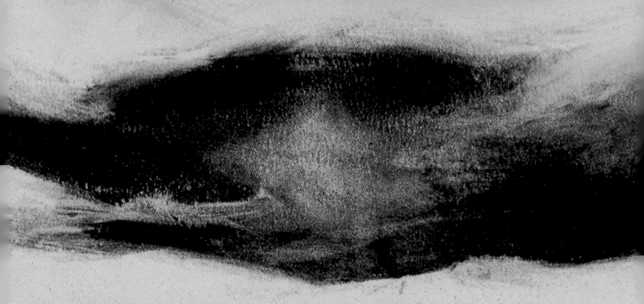

into memory

I will never persuade anyone
that we met

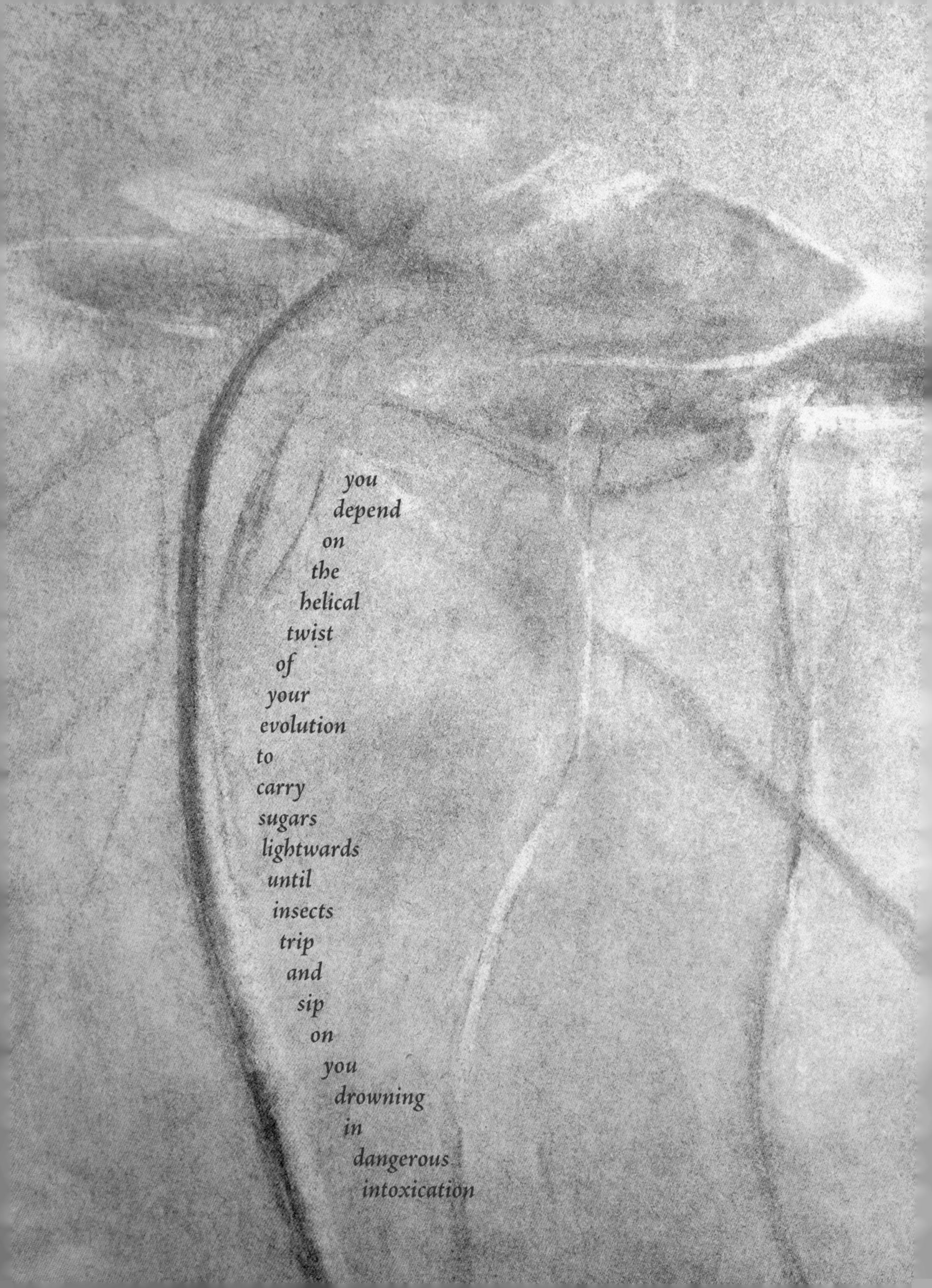

you
depend
on
the
helical
twist
of
your
evolution
to
carry
sugars
lightwards
until
insects
trip
and
sip
on
you
drowning
in
dangerous
intoxication

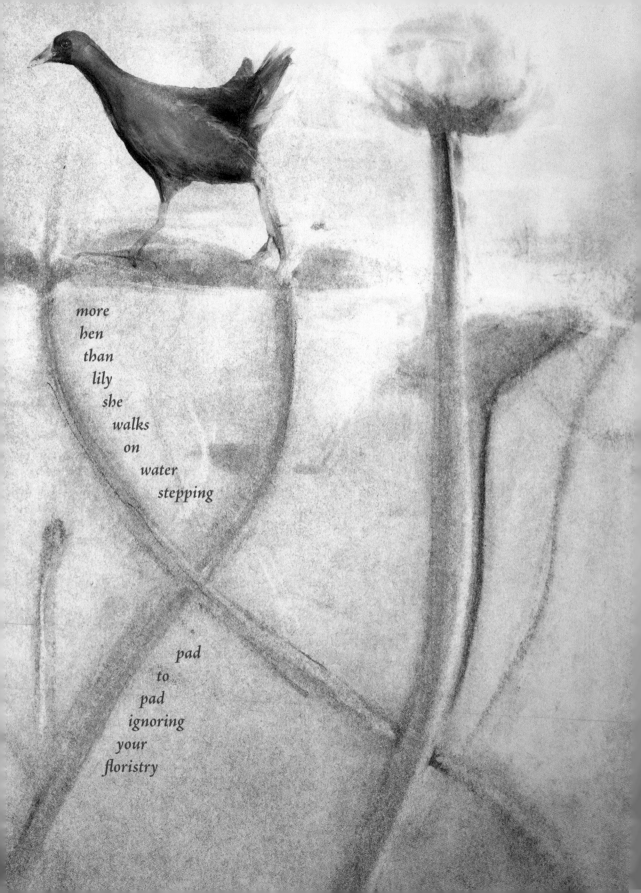

more
hen
than
lily
she
walks
on
water
stepping

pad
to
pad
ignoring
your
floristry

water-crowfoot

if you dive deep
into this sargasso
of freshwater kelp
you will find
entanglements
and now above
a living mat of flowers
that only the lightest
can walk upon

she keeps her
water-crowfeet rooted
in ice-age worn
gravel, stone and pebble
through deeps and
shallows
of chalk and limestone

if you follow
the eddies
and swirls of her
language
you'll see the longest
milk-white words
she knows
how to write
the infinite names
of her
many
children
curving
into
the
flow

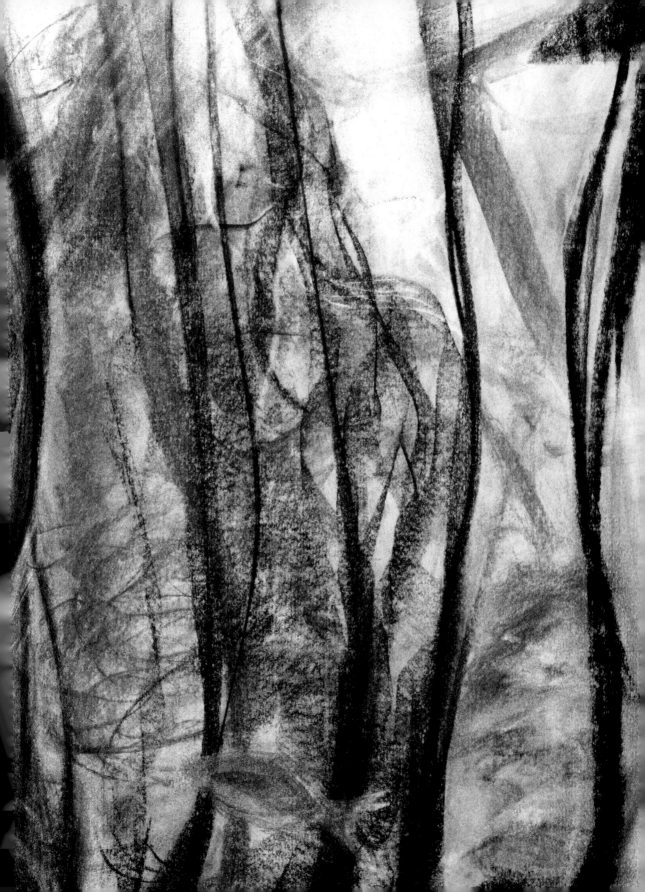

pike

incompletely
walton called you 'tyrant'
and some might say
you're lurksome
waiting
still
as you do

a surreal camouflage
oily greens and yellows
by magritte
against a canvas
of tumble-reed

'ceci-n'est pas un brochet'
whisper the naiads
yet to hatch
into their
emerald and sapphire
above-world winged colours
safe in knowing
you will pay them
small attention

nothing disturbs
in your zen-still smurk
not now you've seen

a sliver of silver

where are the flowers which grew on the mede?

fix your spills and waste-water crimes?

the cat's-ear, vetch, the daisy, knapweed

they followed the river, they made it sublime.

are you going to?

are you going to mend and play fair?

    fix your spills and waste-water crimes?

        remember nature once she was there.

  her river once was a true love of mine.

    the future is ours and nature's to hold

      fix your spills and waste-water crimes?

        we're bringing an end to lies that you've told.

  our river once more a love for all time.

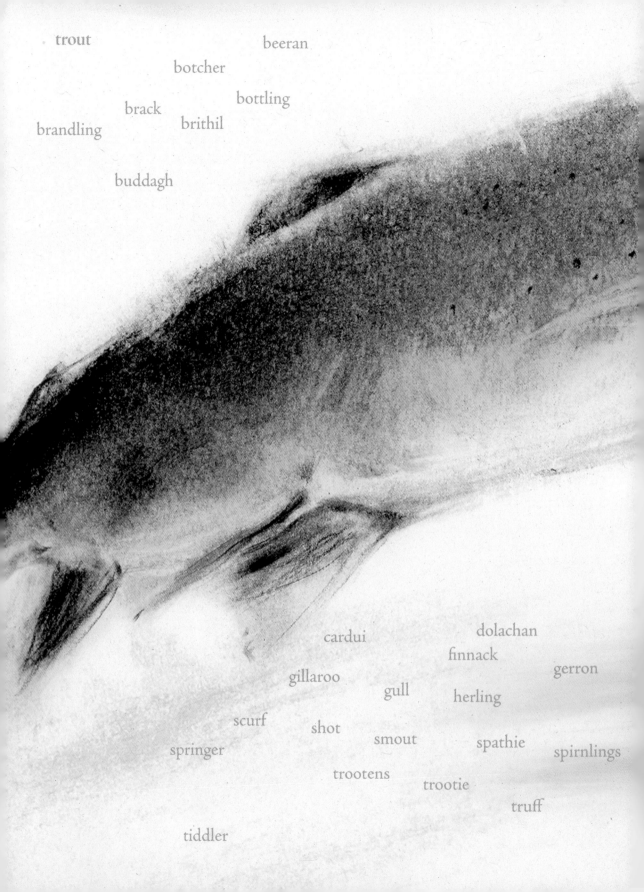

trout

beeran

botcher

bottling

brack

brithil

brandling

buddagh

cardui

dolachan

finnack

gillaroo

gerron

gull

herling

scurf

shot

smout

spathie

springer

spirnlings

trootens

trootie

truff

tiddler

caddis-fly

once sand-grains, twigs
and stones
were bound by silken thread
these things no longer found
along the river's bed

the caddis nymph now
hunts
through detritus misplaced
human waste and plastics
are all that it can paste.

a cotton-bud, elastic band
a micro-bead or three
her tiny life of gathering
diminishing to see

if we don't prevent it
there's more at stake than this
the salmon, trout, and dipper
are also things we'll miss

our homes we've made
of brick and tile
keep elements at bay;
without us taking action
then nature's flushed away

kingfisher

in halcyon days
goddess Iris
laboured to give birth

in emergence
your beak mistook
the diaphragm of her eyes
for a glint
of fish

blindly
she fired you
newly fletched
with blues and golds
torn
from still damp sky
from her rain-bow

today
as you shuttle back and forth
along the warp of river and trees
your weft of blue thread
stitches
an ever-changing cloth
of heaven

old man willow

you are older than the mole-hills
satelliting
your bankside roots

the laughter lines of your face
are inhabited
by your friends: moss and liverwort
casually
they've also put down roots
to hear the best tales on the riverbank
and anyway
you're not going anywhere
for now

willow tits hop, and whisper,
and gossip into your hair
which is long
you old hippy, you

it's time perhaps, to give you
a number one trim
to gather it in thick whips
from bud to tip
it'll grow back
it always has

if we burn
these leavings
gently
slowly
we can turn these swept back twigs
into charcoal

if you wait for me, i will make a drawing
a drawing of you in your youth
each grey textured stroke
like a patient wave
of willow hair
in the spring breeze

collier

scare-devil

jack

flit

screamer

swing

whip

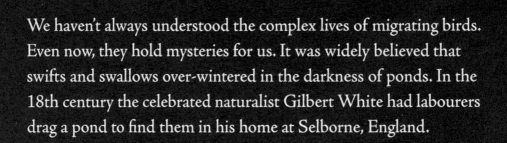

We haven't always understood the complex lives of migrating birds.
Even now, they hold mysteries for us. It was widely believed that
swifts and swallows over-wintered in the darkness of ponds. In the
18th century the celebrated naturalist Gilbert White had labourers
drag a pond to find them in his home at Selborne, England.

water-touching

wing spirals

swift

snatches

mayfly

ephemeral

life

auguries of iciness

to see the world all dewy-paned
and heaven in an hour
by cherwell's bank with hoar frost stained
glass bauble for a flower

willow's loom, a lattice made
above the water's skin
woven threads in brightened shade
a forming jewel within

far below the chub and trout
in wonderment they gaze
with wordless voice: 'look' they shout
swim water-bound, amaz'd

the tit, a moorhen, and old jack
all flap in raptured dream
as all the brightest orbs astack
above the cherwell stream

otter, stoat, and muntjack tell
the words of winter's song
woodpecker plays transparent bell
as river flows along

it's warmer now, the baubles hang
reflecting light and sound
each drip of ice a lasting pang
of memory to ground

Would I were, in Grantchester, past
   Where river flowed, so clean, so fast
Some, once-upon a may-have-been,
   With Nature's pastoral river scene.

Lord Tennyson notes, with grievous eye,
   The slurried, Cambridge waters nigh
Wordsworth, Coleridge, Hughes and Plath
   No more will cross its word-wide path.

Virginia Woolf dipped skin right here
   With Rupert Brooke, in waters clear
Their bodies cold, pure wildness gone
   Just ripples left in river's song.

Yet! I will pack, and take a train
   Of memory, to older riverscapes again!
For England's waterways once knew,
   Of insect, plant, and fish, it's true.

Meandered, riverine, land, and fen
   Where we with Splendid Hearts still yen
For Youth, and Childhood, trusting care
   Has turned, through fault, to NeverThere.

Lithe children paddled, as in a dream,
   By bosky wood, in slumbrous stream.
We bathed this way, and dreamt at night,
   Of what came to pass, and how to fight.

Deep meadows fail, and late recalls
   The lies, untruths, the scene appals
Stands the Church clock at ten to three?
   How can there still be honey for tea?

Words by Tony Davis

Tony is an artist, poet and campaigner. He co-founded A Blackbird Sang with environmentalist Genny Early. They both create nature-inspired work in their Oxfordshire studio.

Tony has mixed poetry inspired by Kath's drawings and other research into the names of things. Using dialect words for the Common Hare he launched the Names of a Hare sculpture at the RHS Chelsea Flower Show 2022.

More poems are available at **artmeetstony.com**

Drawings by Kath Fotheringham

Kath is an aquaphile and inspired by her love of wild swimming, the river, its creatures and places, she draws to capture movement and feeling with charcoal. She also works as a graphic designer and open water guide.

Kath's drawings and other work is available at **swimtheriver.com**.

Prints

Eco-digital prints based on the book are available at **ablackbirdsang.com**

Notes on the poetry, text, and drawings

Inside cover

Extract from the poem 'Afon Wysg/Our River Usk'. The final version will alternate between English and Welsh. The River Usk is a unique river habitat in Wales feeding into the River Severn Estuary. Much of its length is designated as SSSI. Sites of Special Scientific Interest (SSSIs) are areas of land and water that we consider best represent our natural heritage in terms of their: flora – i.e. plants. fauna – i.e. animals. geology – i.e. rocks. geomorphology – i.e. landforms. However, like many rivers, the riverscape and the flora and fauna are at risk from poor management by water companies and agricultural practices.

Mountain stream: Rain to Sea

An exploration of words which describe this in the British Isles. Perhaps water is the way that the mountains, hills and landscape talk to the sea.

Minnow

As a river develops the life which begins has the smallest but most astonishing physical expression. These are fish of childhood memory. They are fiercely territorial. If the river-bed gravels deposited in the last ice-age are clear enough then they spawn here with some males dramatically changing colour during the process.